NATURE IS IN EVERYTHING

POEMS

Praise for *Nature is in Everything*

Alexander Olomo's first book of poetry evokes the exhilarating mental landscape of a youth. His poems traverse the elemental dimensions of human experience (night, day, rain, sunlight) seen through the prism of a particular consciousness in a particular place (Ibadan, Nigeria). In '*Yellow Wake*', as the sun rises and 'mothers bribe their kids with *puff-puff* to go to school', the poet reflects: 'maybe the world is a display of *Egungun* stunts'. This sharply observed sense of locality is combined with occasional references to the world of Greco-Roman antiquity that Olomo studied as an undergraduate. In '*When the Rain was not My Friend*', the poet, remembering his mother's spankings, wonders 'if her hands were beaten into strength by Vulcan'. Such moments are among the many charms of this promising debut collection.
— **Luke Roman**, *Professor, Department of Classics, Memorial University, Canada.*

The teaser in *Nature is in Everything* is precisely locked in the magic of that near semiotic overload captured in language, imagery and title.
— **Sola Olorunyomi**, *Professor of Comparative Literature and Cultural Studies, University of Ibadan, Ibadan, Nigeria.*

Alexander Olomo's "*Nature is in Everything*" is a powerful debut collection that celebrates the aesthetics of the natural world. It's a collection whose exquisiteness is anchored by the poet's ability to transport us through the vast landscapes of the world. Poem after poem, the poet unravels the joy of being in a world that offers us the grace of being humans and of waking up to experience the love of nature. Infusing both individual and collective experiences into the poems, the poet acknowledges who we are as humans, while also inviting us to see the astonishing world of rain, sun, moon, birds, mountains, hills, and others. This is a poet to watch out for, as this book is an important announcement of his arrival.
— **Rasaq Malik Gbolahan**, Author, "*No Home in This Land*" and "*The Other Names of Grief*".

NATURE IS IN EVERYTHING

POEMS

Alexander Olomo

ISBN: 978-978-60718-3-1

Published in Nigeria by
Winepress Publishing

Winepress Publishing
Suite 223, Ogun-Oshun River Basin Development Authority, Opposite Palms Shopping Mall, Off Oni Memorial Children's Hospital, Ring-Road, Ibadan
Telephone: +234 809 816 4359, +234 909 666 4359
Email: hello@noirledge.com | Website: www.noirledge.com
Socials: www.linktr.ee/noirledge

Winepress Publishing is an imprint of Noirledge Limited. For information regarding discounts on bulk purchases and special editions of our titles, please contact our Sales Department via: hello@noirledge.com or +234 809 8164 359.

Cover Design: Dhee Slyvester
Book Design: Servio Gbadamosi
Typesetting: Rukayat Amudah
Editorial Team: Utibe Hanson, Ogungbenro Solomon

Dedication

I dedicate this book to my father—Anthony Kolawole Olomo, the one who constantly equips me with teachings necessary for my poetic life and to my mother—Betty Adenike Olomo for constantly demonstrating to me, the importance of hard work by the life she leads.

Acknowledgment

I acknowledge Nature which has always been my muse.

Contents

What is Nature?

What is Nature?
I ask myself this question.
A question that sends my mind on an epic journey.
Nature, like life, difficult to define.
Some say Nature is God and God is Nature.
Some say Nature is created by God.
Some call it the force that controls all.
To me, Nature is many things:
The yellow and orange Sun
The white-full or crescent Moon
The white and dark clouds
The rainbow of colourful cities.
Nature, the sky-birds, and tree-birds.
Nature, the dark forest of cold leaves.
Nature, the expansive waters.
Nature, the dark-brown-red soil.
Nature, the cold-whistling breeze.
Nature, the ever frightening-bullying thunder.
Nature, the ravaging wind.
Nature, the ever- burning-consuming fire.
Nature, the towering mountains with misty zeniths.
Nature, the spread of the blue Sky.
Nature, the physical world.
Nature, the world within.
Nature, the gentle, truth-speaking conscience.
Nature, the mind.
Nature, sound.
Nature, silence.
Nature, what regulates life in its order.
Nature, the force that forms and controls all.

Yellow Wake

Yellow wake, cradle of a new day.
Yellow wake, prologue of the day.
Like bubbles disengaging in their senility, my dreamland experience
dissolves in the opening of my soul into the space of a novel day.
The skyline, light blue.
Uniform complexion across.
This Sky, a homozygous twin to a school of uniformed kids.
This Sky, also like a plain-white paper, waiting to be tattooed by the
labour of a servile pencil.
This Sky, also like a plain white paper, waiting to be populated by a
nation of letters.
Mango trees and palm trees want to touch this beauty.
But none can feel the skin of the Sky.
The Sky restricts them from straying into its territory.
Playful birds, kites of flesh and wings are on vacation.

The Sun cracks through its shell, like a hatching egg.
Rays fight through the blue clouds, like roots pushing through dark
humus.
Brown roofs of *Ibadan* prepare their iron bodies for the daily task of the
Sun.
Sleeping leaves yawn awake.
Medicine men harvest them into bowls.
The Sun, a celestial yoke on the blue dome.
It starts to smile like an *Ibadan* boy watching the *egugun* festival.
Wait! Maybe the world is a display of *egungun* stunts.
Doesn't it have different shades of colour too?
Doesn't it have rhythm?

Grandma Juliana sits on a wooden chair with the shape of a collapsing
letter 'K'

Her *Ankara wrapper,* over ageing breasts of relaxed muscles like a
poster loosening its grip on a wall.
In her mouth, chewing stick diminishes like a pencil suffering the fate
of consistent sharpening.
She recalls her childhood mornings of water-fetching exercises at the
community stream.
The Sun is light-yellow now and mothers bribe their kids with *puff-puff*
to go to school.

Silence

Sometimes, Nature speaks in silence.

Silence, first depicting itself to us as if it is empty like the shell of a snail without the snail.

But verily, it conveys messages.

Silence can be like the banana-conveying-*Ogbomosho* lorries, carrying ideas, thoughts, messages, and visions.

Silence can also be like a road sign, directing motorists and pedestrians to their destination.

Silence, a dart that shoots us to the inner quarters of our minds.

Silence, my mother's state, before slapping the after-school-playfulness out of me.

With silence, men can fetch the sketch of their dreams.

Silence, the telephone line through which the nine daughters of Zeus communicate with mortals.

Silence, the fuel of nature, sustaining and fuelling our existence.

Silence, the colour of a graveyard.

Silence, chaos to the ear.

Silence, nothing.

Silence, something.

Silence, so many things.

Silence, few things.

Silence, an estate where the respect of men for men lies.

Silence, a world in a world.

Silence, a world outside a world.

Silence, historic.

Silence, a coward.

Silence, the carcass of sound.

Silence, a lifetime.

Silence, silent.

With silence, Nature tells us about itself.

With Nature, silence tells us about us.

Childhood Nights

Mother held the night lantern.
Its nucleus, yellow, like the morning Sun.
Its handle, warm, like mother's bosom that flourishes with affection.
Its top, dark, like thick forests.
The night lantern, a mobile fireplace of warmth.
With the night lantern, I did my assignments.
I feared having my juvenile buttocks flayed with hell-spirited canes.
In the regard of assignments, I was like a young lover wooing a damsel
of first-class appeal with all zeal on success.
With the night lantern, we learnt how to be friends with playful, butter-
colour-compact butterflies that turn our lantern to a museum.
Memories drag back nights of my childhood in Ibadan.
With bare chests and a rotund young belly, I studied at nights while eyes
functioned like epileptic power supply.
Knocks from mother reminded me of the future promised to her by me.
Some nights were spent on the balcony and while I waited for mum and
dad, the wind brought the call of my name to my sleepy self.
During some childhood nights, I strolled with father while my tender
legs threw my body into intermittent jumps, a representation of a
thrilling experience.
There was the Moon, Stars of flourishing brightness and breezy delight
of folktales.
On some nights, burning tears brimmed mother's eyes, eroding her
happiness as asthma endangered hopes of me growing into a man.

Though electricity was like a strayed dog during my childhood nights,
nature lit my heart with hope and assurance for the desired future.
Though a juvenile, the nights of my childhood were virile.

Raindrops

Like the fall of grains, rain drops.
It marches with its cold feet in the air.
Moving with noisy speed, the feet of men chase shelter.
Daylight is excusing.
Average darkness, the blanket that covers my town.
In complete wetness, the wings of local fowls lose the power of flight.
Though, in full remembrance of mothers' whip, boys and girls run into the rain for the sweet whipping of the drops.
When the rain drops, we no longer care about our taps.
When the rain drops, we do not care about pneumonia even though we knew its rule is quietly waiting for us like the tape at the end of a finish line in a marathon race.
Drenched in the rain, fathers returned with hopes for dinner.

Nature Never Forgets Me

There were days I got comfort the harder I cried.
There were days I sealed my letter to Nature with tears.
But I know that one day, I shall wake up with a happy Sun within me.
The Sun will emerge again.
The Moon will play in the Sky soon.
The Stars will appear once more.
The bright rainbow will come out again.
My tears will be washed by the rain.
The muddy soil will soon be stronger.
This hope will soon be incubated as the present, for I know Nature
never forgets me.
I know I shall soon be fuelled by joy that I shall wish to dance in a bottle.
Nature never forgets me.

Bright Night

Bright night Sky.
Song of the Moon.
Sing to my eyes.
I hope my lover can see you too.
Moon! Moon! Moon!
Keep this night going.
That I may not be in the dark.

Morning Rain

In foggy parachutes, the drops land safely.
Cold Rain wraps my being like a candy.
Even my will to work is wrapped too.
The morning Rain is a manipulator.
The morning Rain is divergent.
The morning Rain is a trickster.
Now, the day, older than its look.
And cold breath inspires the mental factory of a poet.
Maybe the morning Rain is my doctor.
Maybe the morning Rain loves me.
This morning Rain, not careless to allow the wind to hijack its mission.
The morning Rain, smart.

Deserted Night

Tomorrow might meet my absence.
Dogs of this night see and flee.
My face, solemn with black rays.
This is a deserted night.
Hope, prematurely dead.
From my empty soul, I ask:
"Why did night come today?"
From my empty soul, I ask Nature whether my village paid not, its dues for joy.

I Saw Hope

I saw hope. Yes, I did!
I mean I saw hope: when it rose with Dawn; when it rose with the novel
Sun, when memories of past moments stopped shedding tears.
The rose garden I stayed with my lover is no more.
 My eyes have lost the virility of their yokes.
Yet, I still saw hope because Nature sponsored my strength to see it.

This Night

This night is quiet.
So quiet for me to remember candles put off by the rain.

This night, calm.
So calm for me to remember candles extinguished by fast tears.

This night, tranquil.
So tranquil for me to recall times that the breaths of men went frail.

This night, with me.
But with the past, it came.

This night, quiet, yet not pacific.
This night, my tears defeat raindrops.

December

Former greens, dry and brown like bones left on the field of time.
The cold morning flogs babies into a feast of tears.
Whizzy! Whizzy!
So is the tune of the era.

Dusty breeze, everywhere.
Raiding the town like a plague.
The fingerprint of cold, seen everywhere.

Where Nature Celebrates Along

Dawn breaks out.
Hearts glitter, for the toil of ages is adorned today.
Let the old beats be flushed out of drums like stale water of a pool.
And let fresh beats be let in.
For today is for songs and dances.
For today is the remembrance of my mortal emergence into this world.
Give red wine to all that inhale and exhale, now that Dusk is rising on its limbs.
Now that it is evening, I can see the Moon and Stars far up there, side by side to honour me.
Nature chose today to be so.

I rejoice and cogitate.
Nature whispers a message to me.
"As a candle shines, its wax diminishes, inch by inch."

Well, one's juvenile and virile epoch is to be enjoyed and cherished immensely.
When I am senile and my Rains go down in quantity and voice, I shall think the way elders at that age think, live the way elders at that age live, say what elders at that age say, sing what elders at that age sing, write about what elders at that age write, smile the way elders at that age smile and tell stories elders at that age tell.
I shall perceive the way elders at that age perceive.
Then, I shall witness the final reality.

My Green World

The morning, clear under a blue Sky.
My green world, all that makes me smile and sing.
The caps of houses, wet.
The breeze, young and understanding.
This morning convinces me of its peculiar fashion.
My will to tame the day is strengthened, minute after minute.

This morning is a green robe of nature.
And I watch men and women sing green songs for it.
I help school kids lace their shoes and I get a smile in reward.
I tell stories of how large the heart of the Sun is, to listening boys and
girls.
I watch people help each other to get up.
Now it is evening, I watch the Rain give its contribution to the rivers on
behalf of mankind.
I watch debtors forgiving the 'sin of debts.'
I notice that every man is a rainbow, clad with different acts of kindness.
Surely, my world is green.

A Night Not Bright Enough

The Moon that once made me read my history is hidden behind the Sky.
I see a night Sky not bright enough.
I can also see the beeping light of a flying plane.
The trees are scary this night.
I tell myself the Moon is on its way.
But I do not know its itinerary.

Where are the Stars?
This Sky, like a shadow
I miss those night tales I tell kids.

Is the Moon seeing me?
Is the Moon astray?
I walk away from my house to find the Moon.
But I find a Star.
It shines, but its light is not bright enough for me to write down my
message for coming generations.
Its light, not bright enough for me to sow what my belly will carry in
coming days.
Its light, not even bright enough for me to lead this wandering boy to
his village.
Its light, not bright enough for me to pour this herbal mix into the
mouths of those who have one leg within and one beyond this world.

Under this moonless Sky, drops race down my eyes of dark experience
unto dust that once bore the feet of dancers.
Under a moonless Sky, only the corpse of joy is left.

On this Muddy Soil

On this muddy soil, I sit.
On this paste of red earth, I cry and remember cloudy days of corpses
and wails.
I know life is like a calendar and expired days and months will leave the
front row.

But why should my friends be hurriedly torn from the calendar of life
and thrown away?
But I know they live in the closets of my heart.

I know I will get up soon.
This muddy soil will soon be stronger.

The Inferno

It gets on the stage of Time like actors of all shades of dialogues and motions.
Running, jumping, flying.
It consumes both things of co-incidence and those that dare to end its reign.
While the act is on, it makes everywhere well-lit for a sorrowful spectacle.
Many things and people existing in this clime are being consumed.

I watch the inferno closely.
I see something in it—the zeal to bring everything to ashes.
The zeal to dominate all.

Not All Mornings Have the Sun

Like a schoolboy stretches out of a duvet, this morning stretches out
from the blanket of night.
This Sky, white as wool.
This Sky, expansive as land.

Another morning has encroached, like a successive king on a throne.
But this morning has no Sun.
Children shake my older hands for an answer to drop.
An answer, I have not.

I sit to re-visit the mental pages of my life's experiences.
Then my answer comes like swift-footed Mercury.
"When you search for Sun in the Sky and find it not, look into your
heart, you will find it there."

Even if the morning doesn't have a Sun, I will set out like a soldier.
I will keep marching till I see where the Sun is waiting for me.
I am a soldier.
I will keep marching till the Sun blazes high in the Sky when victory is
decorated and celebrated.

I Am Not Sure But I Am Sure

I am not sure of the Sky's complexion when I announced my
appearance in this world.
I am not sure of my birth date.
I am not sure if evening birds flew in the Sky that minute.
I am not sure the Sky was without Moon that night.

But I am sure there was a Sky on that day.
I am sure the Moon shone on subsequent nights.
I am sure I was fed with mother's milk on that day.
I am sure some bowls of water were sacrificed to clean my blood-
stained body.
I am sure the freshness of the air that strayed in, through my window,
fanned me to sleep on that day.
I am sure the songs of birds replaced my mother's songs as lullaby,
sometimes.
If I am not sure of how Nature was on my birthday, I am sure of Nature's
existence ever since then till now.
Even when I die, I am sure Nature will care for my body.

When the Sun is a Spear

When the Sun is a spear, it adds to the challenges of a sad and lonely man.
Cries have tales.
Tales of tears can remove the badge of courage.
In the depth of sorrow, my spine gives in to aches.
The space, an enemy that I am alone with now.
Terrible journeys of stunted beginnings.
Harrowing ends of wailings.
Sunshine, a spear now.
My sleep, a past that goes farther into the chambers of time.
The floor where my burning feet once sought succour is the harbour of torment, making my feet the town of scars.
Let someone tell Sun that I can crawl.
I am a sad poet.
My only haven, the poem I write, even though they push out more tears.
I will keep on with my poems on this spot that life has planted my existence.

Yuletide

It is harmattan.
My eyes welcome yuletide.
These kids around me chuckle and laugh.
Cathedral bells are calling.
Now, hymns swirl skyward.
Joyful renditions about yuletide tickle quiet birds into tunes.
I see men and women, clad in red and white on the field with beautiful
gifts confidently reflecting Sun rays.

It is night.
The Moon inspires me to tell tales to these lads.
Tales of soldiers led home by alcohol for Christmas.
Tales of my past yuletides come.
It is night.
Bulbs are of various colours like the paraphernalia of a masquerade.

Under Sunshine

Under sunshine, I love to smile a lot.
I feel my heart is working under a bright light.
Under sunshine, I was alone for a long time like a sick dog.
Under sunshine, I met her.
Under sunshine, I always want to play with her.
Honestly, her beauty doubles under sunshine.
Whatever I say under sunshine is trustworthy.

At the Riverbank

Tonight, a night of songs.
Thunder rumbles and grains of rain fall all through a lengthy route.
Tonight, I blow my flute at the riverbank and speak to the souls of the
ages to come.
My songs speak of loneliness.
The essence of the world depreciates in loneliness.
The essence of the world can appreciate in loneliness as well.
I will continue to mingle with my flute.
As I blow, hope brightens like the eyes of Athena.

Graveyard Birds

The conversation of graveyard birds creates a night disturbance.
I stand on the sandy path and watch the cries of big-eyed owls sketch
lamentations round me.
Is it not enough that this night is not bright?
My watch beeps and my sadness take another medal.
The pains in the hearts of these birds have become a heap.
The leaves of these trees bow and shake heads like warriors under
defeating daggers.
These minutes are in torn robes of peace.

Let someone call pastoral seers who will blow stories and the tears of
these birds will go away.
Let someone call pastoral seers who will blow stories and my tears will
go away.

August Rain

Oh! The constellation is gone, taking the blue Sky along and leaving the dark one behind.
I mean that one that is as dark as a forest without light.
It is the command they must obey.
For the 'master' has come and everyone runs here and there.
Like hare and deer.
Even children are out to bathe and writers are waiting for the inspiration that it has brought.
But I am here, standing on my desire.
With a broad heart, I want a cold bed that will bring good dreams closer to me.

These raindrops are reincarnated past.
Now I know the Rain can be an old man with didactic tales.

Petals

Petals of curly lips.
Petals of soft lips.
My eyes harvest petals of various colours.

Some are red.
Some are white.
Some are yellow.

My soul is tired, and my lashes drown in the sea of tears.
I am tired of plucking fruits of sorrows.
I am tired of watching these petals.
Even if I cry more, I shall pick some to lay my tears to rest.

Farewell to Night

Farewell to night.
Day stretches its arms.
Farewell to night.
Its eyelids are no longer heavy.

Farewell to night.
I hear the voice of the town crier blaring like a siren.
Farewell to night.
For the Sky is no longer thick in darkness.

Farewell to night.
For the Sun now sits on the throne of day with his sceptre of command
and a crown of honour.
Farewell to night.
For the Moon and the Stars are behind the curtain of the Sky.
And they sobbingly say: '-our night-play is over'.

Farewell to night.
My body is strong now.
Everywhere I turn to, I see not, the remains of night.

The Rain Will Come

Fellow villagers,
When we hurl curses at the Rain like Spartan hands hurling spears,
Our children are learning the chorus.
They will sing well to future sorrow,
Perhaps, to our death;
Maybe to theirs as well.

Let somebody tell the rain maker he is no champion.
The Rain will come, not by cursing the Sun.
The Rain will come, not by dry leaves, fire, flames, and air-bearing
incantations.
The Rain will surely come.

Dark Rain

This night is dark.
So, is the rain.
I sit on this wet soil as my forehead and my knees are in a conjugation.
Slowly, memory covers me with a blanket and memories descend on my being.

Memories regurgitate tears.
Memories regurgitate silence.
Memories control.
Memories teach.

That Night

That night, when I fell prey to the mutiny of dust and cold, my breath
became short like a skimpy skirt of a lady.
Dizziness became a refugee in the district of my head.
The breeze came to me, but my skin enjoyed it not.
Sweats turned me to a leopard.
My body melted in pain, and it seemed like nature wanted to take my
spirit out of my body like an orange taken out from a sack.
That night, I thought I was going to be another fallen leaf on the tree of
life, but I was like a river drying up only to be filled again by the rain.

Upward to the Sky

Upward to the Sky, I look.
For that is where my world is now.
I will henceforth look and write my poetry.
I will keep writing and reciting my poems to the Sky.
Hopefully, the Sky will pour down its water to calm my stress and wash my tears down my cheeks.
I know the Sky is always appreciative of poets.

I have studied the Sky for a long time, and I know that the Sky is like a human being.
When it wants to smile, the Sun comes down.
When it wants to cry, the Rain shows up.
When it wants to shout, the Thunder rumbles.

I have studied the Sky.
I have nothing more to say to men.
I shake my head and enter my mind.

Dawn

Dawn is not only when the elevator of time raises the Sun and its rays
like a lover with a gift on an escalator.
Dawn is not only when sleeping plants wake.
Dawn is not only when the muezzin calls out for prayers.
Dawn is not only when cocks of red crowns stubbornly shout.

Dawn is also when my eyes close their lids into the memory of love.
Such a dawn is always replenishing.
Dawn is also when I watch an Austrian orchestra and hold my lover's
hand passionately.
Dawn is when I say 'goodbye' to my lover and later say 'hello' with a
poem of romantic darts.

Dawn is a continuum of many nuances.
Dawn can be love.
Dawn is always inspirational.

Cold

The rain I wish to have later has jumped over the walls of its imprisonment, casting darts from above.
The sound of the drops makes those on the street hopeless about an early home arrival.

Seers calm these mothers.
On the street, legs are very fast, but the white lightning is faster.
When the lightning flashes, I see the lofty cross of a nearby chapel.
I lay on my couch, cold, lost, and helpless.

I Shall

When the fire burning within the chambers of the heart of raindrops goes high like a burning ember preparing to replenish their passion, I shall poke my lover's nose with my thumb.
Her dimple will appear once again.
Then, I shall lay my lips on her temple.
Then, I shall touch her scarf and let time disappear into the warmth of our embrace.

The Trio

I remember your presence in my land.
When time was vertical.
And when time was horizontal.

Rain, Wind, and Lightning!
Are you cowards?
Your absence has drawn me under the servitude of tears and cries like a
djinn.

Hurry, you trio!
Wind, blow these cries away.
Rain, sweep these tears away.
Lightning, scare them far beyond Styx into Tartarus where they belong.

Where is Wind?
Where is Rain?
Where is Lightning?

The New Sun

Rattling pains in my heart are struggling to woo me.
I listen to the muddy path.
Rough! Delicate! Soft!
It frowns at my booted feet.
Ah! Life is a field of torment and a garrison of hopeless posterity but not
when the new Sun swims out of the cold blue ocean.
Comrades, let our voice cry out to the singing birds to relinquish
crumbs of loaves into our thick, bloody palms.
Certainly, we are beggars.

Comrades! Oh! Comrades.
In this forest, our steps are slow, but tears are fast, faster than racing
hares.
On the plains, for the concern of their bellies, bugs suck nectars
conglomerated with robust drops.
They leave us to our fate.

Voices of Flame

Young we are, but not too young to hear the gong of death.
On these pyres, fire dances by the energy of shinning oil.
The naked bruises tell the tale of woe.
Babies cry no more, for the time is odd.

Somebody tell the elders that no one is young where the carnival of death rocks the streets.

We may be puerile, but we know these calabashes are black and the diviners are chanting the songs of shades.

Alas! Today is not that for the living.
The rooms where we get succour have been locked forever.
Fellow companions! This is a feast where vultures are seen all over.
Let us not wipe this blood away for with it, we shall remember this carnival like the tale of a deserted city is always told.
Nature has placed flame in our voices.

Back from Slumber

Back from slumber, the Thunder silences the barking dogs.
It rains and these hungry children run to her hut, but the *akara* seller
has gone beyond the clouds.
Ah! The only succour we lick and enjoy has evaporated from our grab.
Of springs of trumpets are going pale like travelling voices.
In the woods of death, trees do not grow tall.
And the reality of living flows down rods of oppression.

The powers of the day purge themselves with bananas of greed.
The shadow of peace shapes our city into Tartarus.
The words of my masters are alive.
But their hearts are dead.

I am back from slumber, but my dreams cannot be told.
Justice was the first to shed and lick tears.

What is Nature doing to lift me from this predicament?
This day, I call for the support of Nature.
May rains of hot scorches pour on my oppressors like hot water falling
on a condemned fowl!
May the Sun burn their clothes of felicitation.
May their Rainbow have one colour.

My New Rain

When you put me in the vehicle called pain and instruct the driver
called Grief to take me far away into the forest, don't join the search
team tomorrow, looking for me.
Hypocrisy, the soil that supports your soul.
The flame that will suffocate your soul is gathering.
My return will be faster than you expected.

I shall return with a new Rain.
What is this new Rain?
Wait!
Wait for the answer that will lie in moments when the evil ones have
their souls governed by flames darker than shadows and that are
standards of ruining fire and the drops of my new Rain will scornfully
march away in yellow and orange cloaks that glow by the language of
the drum, never to extend a helping hand.

My Grandma, My Earth

Nature is an artisan; we are her arts.
Nature is the force that puts everything into becoming.
Becoming, as each inch of time extends.
Nature is the regulating scope of a man's existence like the lines of a
pitch.
Nature is the regulating scope of a man's existence like laws of punitive
robes.

The earth is part of nature.
The earth is a stakeholder in the management of life.
Bringing forth men like Zeus.
Sustaining the soul and feet of men.
Taking in the residue of men.
The earth guides.
The earth forgives and gives.
The earth multiplies given input.
The earth absorbs.
The earth, synopsis of a man's world.

My grandma, my nature.
My grandma, my earth.
Grandma, today is for adulation because you live on.

My Assured Return

See, I won't drown.
This river, taking me away on your instruction.
Another will return me in a new robe on the instruction of my fate.
Your scornful hypocrisy is about to twist its waist to the rendition of the
song of regret.
Evil men, these lines of dirge you prepare for my innocent soul will be
recited at your funeral and repeated at those of your children, like
words that were not heard the first time.
The river, my friend.
I will return.

The Betrayers

I know a tree and a bird.
They are fond of each other just like a mother and a child.
The bird whistles melodious songs while the tree dances.
The tree is always faithful to the bird.
The bird is always faithful as well.
They are both faithful to me.
I come here every day so that the dry leaves of my life can fall off.

Ah! See my kinsmen cutting the tree with their chainsaw, they cut down
my link to nature's message for me.
My kinsmen are betrayers.

My New Sky

From boyhood till adulthood, the Sky has been my friend.
I dive into pacifism when it wears the blue robe with the wool-like clouds.
Even when the Sky is dark, it is for my sake.
It pours me great drops of happiness.
The Sky has always been my suspended theatre of marvellous shows performed by the yellow Sun, white Moon, and the twinkling and glowing Stars.
I have met Aduke, and she becomes my new Sky.

Who says she isn't my Sky?
Let him come see the comeliness of her character.
He should come notice how she stays with her friends and never strays away.
He should come watch the magnificent spread called her face.
He should come enjoy the sight of the glittering pendants Nature placed on her face.
Her face, a Sky, my new Sky.
Her face, a new Sky giving me sunshine, moonlight, rainfall, and starlight.

Refined Morn

The morn is refined, like bathed baby.
I will rise to the hills with my lover.
There, creamy affection is pre-destined to stand.
I shall run with her to the streams of melodious nymphs where we shall
rub our backs with smooth waters.
On Helios's cattle, we shall tear a feast and our love will spread rays.

Along the Boulevard

Along the boulevard, I walk, head bowed.
And my spirit follows suit as I converse first with it, then with my silence.
I see no breath in this evening where I have a soliloquy rather than dialogue.
Many things strangle my happiness.
The tears of lost poetry flow down my cheeks.
This evening, I live in past days.

Along the boulevard, the streetlights of my heart switch off one after the other.
The city is illuminated, like a night of a full Moon.
But my world within is dark and nasty with thoughts and experiences.

Along the boulevard, I walk with one prayer – never to have memory of unpleasant events.
I gather a tribe of sand and pour on my head to bury those ugly thoughts in my head but around the corner, I see, lovers playing into each other's world.

Along the boulevard, I hold my head and scream of a bleeding night.
Along the boulevard, I kiss my fate.
Along the boulevard, I walk home.

Nature's Trick

Night of sad tales.
The Moon walks us home when the Stars leave us but no offence we
carry.
The Stars are our friends too.

Hope, like Rain.
Some days, we have it.
Some days, we do not.
Yesterday, no Rain.
Today, Rain on Rain.
A trick we need to learn.
The Rain is our friend too.
In our friends, many colours dwell.

The Afternoon Breeze

I sit on this green chair, close to my window.
This is an afternoon where the Sun and the breeze are fond of each other.
I can see the fingers of the pawpaw tree tolerating the disturbance of the breeze.
The breeze tears into my space and woos me.
The tunes from my room connive with the breeze to form an afternoon's road map that leads me into remembrance.
I am an onlooker on the street of past events.
Sometimes, time can be a code breaker, explaining life.
I look at these rusted roofs and it becomes clear that time is the paddle of the canoe of life.
I cycle into a gaze and some drops fall.
Now, my paper has lost some inhabitants.
The memory of less refined acts teaches a man the essence of cherishing anything called the present.
Returning to my chair in consciousness, I sob.

Crux of My Sensations

A circle drawn by chalk in the evening, splits when the morning dew spreads everywhere.
My sensations may not possess a consuming speed that can weed an old man's garden, but the direction is there.

When the Rain was not My Friend

I was as young as a day at its shinning era when I knew the rain was not my friend.
I got the message from the spanks that mother's hands gave me.
I wondered if her hands were beaten into strength by Vulcan.
I wondered why she said the Rain wasn't my friend.
The Rain wanted me, and I wanted it.
We wanted each other like a magnet and a screw want each other.
The Rain loved to bounce on my small head and then roll down my face.
The Rain loved to make my worn clothes heavy.
The Rain also loved to switch on the difficulty in my breathing just like an appliance is switched on.
Mother would release burning drops from her eyes and tell me the Rain was not my friend, in a voice that struggles for clarity.
When the time of labour was over for me, the Rain would lure me again.
Truly, the Rain was not my friend.

Not Every Bird

Not every bird is evil.
Not every bird spoils a healing medicine.
Not every bird will tear down the house of hope with a sad song.
Not every bird is horrible to children.
Not every bird does stink like the anus of a monkey.
Not every bird prevents men from enjoying the bliss of eating their mangoes.
Not every bird. Not all of them.
Some birds know how to fly and sing well for us to watch and listen.
Birds are beautiful flying arts of God.

I Look

I look at the canoe harboured at the riverbank, and I remember dreams
that were dropped by the roadside of life.
I look at the reflection of light on the river and I remember the
afternoon Sun that attends the funeral of men that wished to live
longer.
I look at the ostracism that nature gave the fallen tree and I sing a dirge
to it.
I look at the wet grass and I remember the tears of mothers on the chest
of boys that could not breathe again.

When the Moon Strays Away

When the Moon strays away, the night turns dark.
When the Moon strays away, it is to give a lesson to us.
When the Moon strays away, we see with the torch of meditation.
The Moon strays away this night and it turns dark like a chalkboard, I write my story on it.
This night is dark, the only light I see is the one my mind convinced my eyes they are seeing after a long time of gazing.
This night is a black book that only memories like smoke are its inhabiting letters.

Arrival of the Beautiful One

I sit, staring at the Moon.
With my eyes, I search for the soul of Elizabeth just as a man looks for his last coin.
Elizabeth was not my last coin.
She was my only coin.
Separation dashed away with my only coin as booty.
Her fleshy presence with me, plundered by herself.
Each day after her demise seems like a deserted village.
Blank and empty.
Worthless and clueless.
Hopeless with teary scenes
Ah! Her absence is a cane that lashes my soul.
But wait!
I am no loner.
I am no loser.
I am a lover.
When I remember her, she is with me like a man's name is plastered to him.
My memory journeys back like a cassette player re-visiting a recording.
Those stories her mother sung to me were stories of her birth.
Stories of the arrival of the beautiful one.
Golden stories.
Invaluable maps of eternal worth, driving me through the knowledge of her advent.
Tonight, she has arrived again in a soft reminiscence.
With my wooden flute, I traverse in the song of her birth.

The first line of Sun ray tore dark clouds.
Light-blue Sky smiled high above her village, our village.
And like a simultaneous band performance, Elizabeth hatched with the emergence of a novel day.

Morning Sun shone differently.
Subtle cry of baby Elizabeth struck the strings of joy in the hearts of
many, to produce melody played out with smiles and laughter.

Elizabeth, your birth, a spoon that fed many with joy.
Elizabeth, your birth, a film of awesomeness.
Your skin, in comeliness.
Soft as beef.
Your eyes, two full Moons.
I call them identical twins.
Elizabeth, at your birth, the prophecy of greatness was fulfilled.
At your birth, goats were glad to die-an honour at your service.
For a birth like yours is scarce like an eclipse.

The Rain is a divine property only the gods of our fate own.
That night, our village was blessed with it while white-dwindling-cloth
shield you from the sharp pangs of cold.

Your naming, cloaked with beauty.
Joy spelt out its name in the meadow of people's hearts.
The entire village, a carnival where dancers stamped feet on yellow
dust.
The entire village, a festival where drums sang happily.
Your naming, awesome like a field of greens.
 Your naming, wonderful as a jazz band.
The moment and subsequent ones were yellow.
Songs appended their signatures into the air.
Your arrival, a prayer that enriched and nourished all in adoration, like
the round big breasts of a nursing mother do to a baby.
Even Nature and her off springs awed.
They loved what they saw.

Kegs of palm wine made smooth, the throats of men.
Pounded yam and bush meat reworked the engine of people's stomach.
Many fed their fate, fat.

Trees danced incredibly to the instructions of the breeze—a repented
wind.
Whizz-whizz-whizz like a whisper, it went.

Rain intervened not.
Sun, mild and soft on our village.
Spiral trains of smoke went to play in the home of the blue Sky.
They stayed and returned not.

Firewood burnt their lives.
Multiplied burns over multiplied burns.
Also, the instruction of the breeze, a repented wind.
Buttocks of pots, deep in hell and breathing out hypnotizing aroma,
irresistible concubine of the nostrils.
Flies ate, drank and they forgot to fly.

Elizabeth, your birth cut the windpipes of battles.
Your birth stopped the hearts of wars.
Your birth commanded foes to take the oath of peace. Pacific!
Your birth skyrocketed Nature's love for the world. Benevolent!
Your birth cured the sick in our village. Therapeutic!
Your birth led by hands, more births. Inspirational!

Sobs and Thoughts

In the tail of the afternoon worthy of the farmer's toil,
that rude knife hurried my calm blood into the pores of the earth.

I am a stranger in the district called love, but my soul knows the name
of every junction and street.

When the singing birds go calm, I will bring back the chanting of a lover
to my mind.
The road is never smooth for the treacherous one.
Even if smooth, it is to destruction.
The war is over, and the victors pass through this wood, homeward.

On this branch, my tears set a pause to their songs.
My sobs raise their heads to the eyes of losses and my tale is told.

They march in silence with caps off, I weep to the pity of monkeys.
They stop jumping, watching.

Elizabeth has gone her way and I sit here, watching the Sun set.

Nature is Justice

One day, the Sun will speak for the oppressed.
One day, the Rain will show superiority to our tears.
The tubers that were not given to us today will be citizens of our barns tomorrow.
A sincere man is the common enemy of corrupt ones.
My joy is that my flute which I made from the reed on the way to the river is louder now.
My joy is the road that I ply alone.
This joy keeps growing in my heart.
Sometimes, I like to live in the forest of loyal trees than to live in the city of evil hearts.
The rain that falls on good men makes them happy.
It makes their land fertile, and makes their beds cold for a night rest.
The rain that falls on bad men makes them bald and floods their farms.
It gives them cold.
Who says the rain isn't justice itself?

Alexander Olomo is a lawyer licensed in Nigeria. He holds a B.A Classics and an LL.B from the University of Ibadan. His poems have been published in The *Trojan Bloom* (University of Southern California's Multilingual Journal) and in the anthology—*Moonlight Songs for Pa Nelson Mandela* (published by the Society of Young Nigerian Writers). He is currently a doctoral student of Classics at the University of Southern California, Los Angeles. He has had his articles published by the *Nigerian Tribune. Nature is in Everything* is his first book.